Zeus Conquers the Titans
The Wrath of Hera

For Immy

First published in this edition in hardback in 2000 by Orchard Books
This edition first published in paperback in 2001

ORCHARD BOOKS
338 Euston Road, London NW1 3BH
Orchard Books Australia
Level 17/207 Kent St, Sydney, NSW 2000

This text was first published in Great Britain in the form of
a gift collection called *The Orchard Book of Greek Gods and Goddesses*,
illustrated by Emma Chichester Clark, in 1997

Text © Geraldine McCaughrean 1997
Illustrations © Tony Ross 2000
The rights of Geraldine McCaughrean to be identified as the author and
Tony Ross as the illustrator of this work have been asserted by them in
accordance with the Copyright, Designs, and Patents Act, 1988

ISBN 978 1 84121 658 4
1 3 5 7 9 10 8 6 4 2
A CIP catalogue record for this book is available
from the British Library
Printed and bound in China

Orchard Books is a division of Hachette Children's Books
www.orchardbooks.co.uk

ZEUS CONQUERS THE TITANS
THE WRATH OF HERA

GERALDINE McCAUGHREAN
ILLUSTRATED BY TONY ROSS

ORCHARD BOOKS

ZEUS CONQUERS THE TITANS

At the very outset of everything, Heaven and Earth had twelve sons and daughters: the Titans. The oldest boy, Cronos, when his hour had come, took his father's throne by force.

Heaven cursed him: "One day your son will take power from you. Then you will taste the sorrow I taste now!"

Desperate to thwart the curse, Cronos swallowed all his own children. All that is, but one, as yet unborn. For his pregnant wife ran away, gave birth in secret, and named the boy Zeus.

Grown to manhood – finding his own hour had come – Zeus rescued his brothers and sisters from the bottomless belly of Cronos and did battle with the Titans, finally hurling them down deeper than the bottom of the universe.

A few lived on, but their Age was truly past. The Age of Olympians had dawned.

Zeus and his brothers shared out the world between them, drawing lots to divide up the prize.

Poseidon won the sea, realm of mermaids, whales and reefs.

Hades won the Underworld with all its gloomy caverns.

And Zeus, shining Zeus won the Upper
World: beach and forest and stream,
continents and islands, deserts
and mountains.

Still Mount Olympus was home to
all three.

Next, Zeus set about peopling the Upper World. First he made a Race of Gold, perfect in form and perfectly happy. They lived from the fruit on the trees, and never fell ill or died.

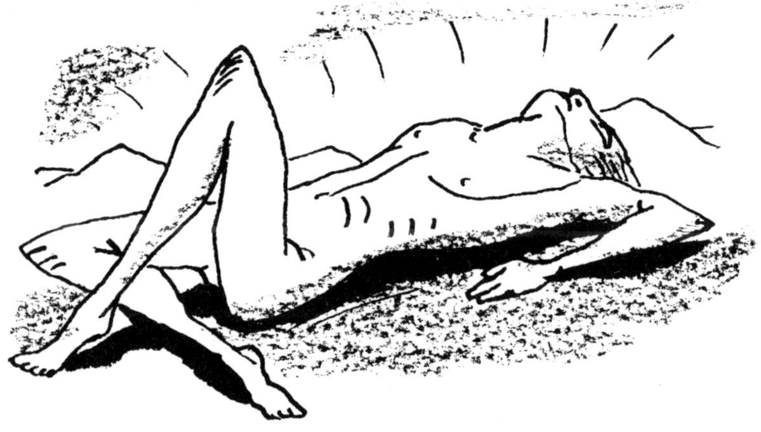

But so easy were their days, so peaceful their nights, that they had a way of sitting down to sleep and not troubling to wake up again. So Zeus-the-Shining melted them down and left only their spirits to watch over the *next* race of people, the ones he cast from silver.

The Race of Silver
were beautiful and
vain. They looked
at themselves in the
dewponds and said, "So
beautiful! We must be gods!"
And so they never turned their silver
faces towards Mount Olympus and, in their
pride, they thought the world was theirs.

So Zeus buried the
Race of Silver in the
ground, and made
the Race of Bronze
instead. They were no
sooner born than they
picked up flints and used
them for tools. They
made axes and spades,
and began industriously
to build. "This is better," said Zeus.

Then they made swords and spears and
arrows and clubs, and left off building to
slaughter one another.
By the time their
war was finished,
Zeus had to begin
all over again.
All that was
left to him was
iron. The Race
of Iron rusted
and grew old.
They worked
and quarrelled,
loved and died.
They worshipped the gods with a fearful
superstition, and bombarded Olympus
with their prayers. In fact they were you.
You Mortals. Humankind. Not much,
but the best Zeus could do with base iron.

All this while, the blood of the Titans Zeus had overthrown lay on the dry, red, red earth. Then, up from the red, red, drops, pushing their ugly faces through the soil, dragging their dragony tails behind them, there came an army of giants. They tore up rocks and trees, and pelted the gods. Hard against Olympus they wrenched up Mount Ossa and balanced it on top of Mount Pelion – a ladder to reach the height of Heaven and attack the Cloudy Citadel.

Their leader, Typhon, was the biggest of
them all, with a hundred heads and eyes
of fire, a hundred forked black tongues
in his hundred gaping mouths.

But Zeus clutched the lightning out of the sky, and thunderbolts from the glowering clouds, and he hurled them at the giants scrabbling up their mountainous siege tower. He rained on them such a hail of noise and light that Ossa and Pelion toppled and crashed, spilling them across the surface of the Earth.

Only Typhon was left standing. The
thunderbolts bounced harmlessly off his
massive chest. The lightning he swatted
away like so many fireflies, laughing.
"You can't kill me, Zeus! I'm immortal
like you, and like you I mean to rule
the world!"

Zeus's hands were empty of weapons;
he had nothing left to throw. With a
hundred barbarous grins, the gigantic
monster came on. "I'll rip you and I'll
eat you. I'll tear you and I'll mince you.
Pull the sea up over your eyes, Poseidon!

Pull the earth up over your head, Hades! You don't want to see what I'm going to do to your brother!"

Then Zeus noticed Italy. It jutted out into the Mediterranean Sea like an icicle hanging from a roof. Now he bent and tore off a piece and, hurling it at Typhon with one last great roaring effort, knocked him far out to sea.

It sank him – a new island – Sicily. And though Typhon struggled and writhed and belched fire from his hundred mouths, his fellow giants could not come to his aid. For the Olympians were piling hills and mountains on top of *them*, burying them under a million tons of rock.

As Typhon had said, they could not die. When they writhe and struggle to break free, molten rock bursts from the mountains over them and bubbles in incandescent rivers down to the sea.

"I want to marry," thought Zeus, as the volcanoes simmered and their noisy eruptions subsided. So he married Metis the Titan, and might have been happy but for something she said one night.

"You know, dear, it is prophesied that you and I will have a child as wise and great as anyone in Heaven," she said dreamily. "As mighty even as you, my love. Think of that!"

Zeus did think. "My grandfather was overthrown by my father. My father I overthrew. What if this child of hers overthrows me?" And opening his mouth, Zeus began to yawn and stretch. The more he stretched, the wider he yawned, and by the time he settled his head on the pillow to sleep he was alone in bed. He had swallowed Metis, prophecy and all. After that, he was often troubled by headaches, but never by any regrets, for there were plenty more women in the world.

✳   ✳   ✳

The goddess Hera heard pecking at
her palace window one winter's day.
She opened the shutters and in fluttered
a tiny cuckoo, shivering with cold.

  "You poor little thing,"
said Hera, her brown
eyes filling with tears.
"Let me warm you."
  Tenderly she
cradled the cuckoo
against the warmth
of her body
and stroked its
ice-speckled wings.
  All day she kept
it with her, and at
bedtime placed it on the pillow by her face.
  All of a sudden, the bed groaned under a
great weight, and the cuckoo disappeared.

In its place, Zeus lay smiling eagerly at Hera and saying, "Kiss me, my beauty."

"Not unless you marry me!" said Hera, rolling quickly out of bed. "I've heard all about you, Zeus! I have a mind to be Queen of Heaven and the one and only love of Shining Zeus!"

So Hera married her cuckoo, and they say the mountains grew a mattress of emerald grass and a quilt of a million flowers to make a fitting bridal bed for the King and Queen of Heaven.

But Hera told him plainly: "I've
heard about you and pretty women.
But from this day forward your kisses
are all for me, understand? Never let me
hear of you wooing
another woman!"

"I will never let
you hear that,"
promised Zeus, eyes
wide and innocent.

But behind his
back he kept his
fingers crossed.

❋   ❋   ❋

Listen! Is that another roll of thunder?
Zeus and Hera are quarrelling again. It
is probably about his philandering. The
truth is, he simply cannot resist a pretty
face. And so his life with Hera has never
been peaceful.

Zeus's children are everywhere and very few of them are Hera's. He has children by mortals,

children by sea nymphs,

children by wood nymphs

and goddesses.

Hermes, messenger of the gods, has flown messages for Zeus time past number – mostly to women. Sometimes Hera tries to destroy his lovers, sometimes just to make their lives a misery. It is a kind of game – like two chess players trying to remove each other's pieces from the board. But Hera plays the game in deadly earnest.

THE WRATH OF HERA

Zeus went to the ends of the Earth to discover where its centre lay. He released twin eagles – one in the east, one in the west. Naturally, the eagles flew towards each other. "Wherever they meet must be the centre of the world," said Zeus, "because they are twins and alike in every way."

Artemis and Apollo were twins as well, but not so very much alike. Zeus was their father, but who was their mother? Hera? Hardly. Metis? Europa? Semele? Old loves long forgotten. No, their mother was Leto the Titan. When Hera heard Leto was expecting twins, and that Zeus was the father, she vowed those babies would never be born. "Earth spare you no space to lie down in, Leto! Time grant you no minute to give birth!"

"Oh but, Your Majesty," protested Leto, "one of them will be Artemis! So like you! Fierce in anger, her arrows sharp – and she will *hate* men!"

"Let her be born, then," said Hera, and Leto gave birth to Artemis. "Who will the second child be?" asked Hera.

"Apollo, bright as the sun!" Leto answered, carried away with pride in her unborn son. "An archer, a sportsman, a lover as handsome as his father..."

"Then the world can do without him
very nicely!" snapped Hera, and she
forbade anyone on earth to show Leto
a friendly face or lend her a kind word.
"Chase her away! Not here, not there, not
anywhere shall Leto find a place to give
birth to her wretched boy-child!"

Leto wept and groaned, walked and
sailed from coastline to island mountaintop.
But people were too afraid of Hera, and
turned Leto away with spits and curses.

"I must rest! I must stop! My baby wants
to be born!"

At last the people of the island of Delos took pity on her. "Rest, lady. Lie down here. Hera cannot forbid what the Fates have decreed. We will be honoured to give your son a home."

So Apollo, the brother of Artemis, was born on Delos, and grew into a youth so handsome that women had only to look at him to fall in love. He spent much of his time riding in the chariot of the sun, bow and arrow in hand, looking for a place to make his home, his Athens, his shrine.

A girl called Clytie caught sight of him one day and fell so deeply in love that she could not take her eyes from his golden face and curling hair and bright, sea-blue eyes. She stood so still that her feet grew into the ground. She stood so long that herbody grew as thin as a flower stalk and her face gold from the flare of the sun. The gods took pity on her and turned her into the world's first sunflower which, even now, turns its face always towards the sun passing overhead, then lets its weary flowerhead fall forwards and drops seeds like tears from a sun-brown face.

Artemis carried bow and arrow, like
her brother. She was a huntress. It did not
matter to her that she was beautiful or that
Apollo was handsome: she did not want
the love of any man. Her train of friends
and servants were all girls, and her only
interest was in chasing the deer, which she
could outrun on her long, lean, brown legs.

One day a mortal hunter called Actaeon
came roaming by, the ground behind him
awash with fifty tumbling deerhounds, all
eager for a scent. Now and then a dog
would throw up its head and sniff – a
rabbit or a wolf. But as yet no deer had
broken cover.

Hearing the bubbling of a river, Actaeon
wondered if he might catch a doe or stag
unaware, drinking at the water's edge. So
softly, without breaking a single twig or
crushing one dry leaf, he wormed his way
through the bushes to see. What he saw
was more intriguing than any deer.

A group of maidens were bathing in the river. Their dresses and bows and quivers hung along the tree branches, their empty shoes all lined up, toe to heel on the bank, they floated idly from one raft of lilies to another flowery weedbed, flicking water into each others' faces and laughing.

At their centre swam the hunter goddess herself, a silver crescent fastening her hair, the sun glistening in every drop of water to roll over her brown skin. Actaeon stared, knowing he should not, but powerless to look away.

Then one of his dogs barked.

Artemis opened her eyes and saw a bush on the bank quivering. "Who's there?"

Actaeon stood up shyly. "I – I didn't mean—"

The sunlight splintered on the water like ice smashed with an axe. The peaceful scene was shattered too, with girls screaming and scrabbling ashore, snatching down their dresses from the branches, quickly dressing. Some were still laughing.

But Artemis was not.

She struck the water with her hand – once, twice, three times. The bush quivered again, and where Actaeon had stood a second before, a big stag trembled, round-eyed with shock. At the very moment Actaeon felt the weight of antlers on his head, his heart experienced the fright of a timid wild thing trapped by hunters.

Artemis did not fire her bow, though her arrows could have felled the fastest animal. Simply to kill the man would have been too kind, as she saw it. For spying on a goddess in her bath, Artemis deemed Actaeon should be hunted down by his own hounds.

He ran – his hoofed feet lent him speed, but his hounds were hungry for the chase.

They came after him slavering, barking,
milling and snarling, climbing over each
other's backs to lay hold on the running
stag. Along the valley and through a wood
of briars and brambles, thickets of sharp
saplings, the terrified creature fled. His
antlers rattled down twigs, his bleeding
flanks left his scent strong and clear on
the barks of the trees.

Fifty deerhounds bayed at his heels as
he broke for the open, head back, breath
too spent for prayers. He ran uphill,
lungs straining, hoofs slipping, feeling
the dogs' hot breath on his
flicking white tail.

He would have shouted out: "Hurricane!
Cyrus! Bella! It's me! Your master!" But
stags are dumb and cannot shout to save
themselves.

Just as he reached the top of a hill,
the dogs overtook him, jaws snapping,
teeth bared... And when they had finished,
nothing was left of the man who had
accidentally offended Artemis.

Leto was right: here was a woman Hera could like! A woman after her own heart. Artemis and the Queen of the Gods became great friends, always exchanging gossip about some foolish thing the male gods had done.

So when one of the hunter maidens of Artemis caught the eye of Zeus, Artemis rooted her out like a weed.

"Go, Callisto! Never call yourself a maiden of mine!"

"Oh but—"

"Go! If you prefer a *man*'s company to mine!"

"Oh I don't, I don't!"

"Run! And see what *Hera* will do to you when I tell her!"

"*No!*"

Callisto ran, as Actaeon had run – not from Artemis but to get help. She ran along riverbanks and through woods, uphill and up mountain slope towards the high home of the gods.

"Zeus! Zeus, help me! My lady Artemis knows! My lady Artemis is going to tell..."

Zeus heard her calling, but so did Hera. The Queen ran to the window and, peering this way and that, tried to catch sight of the loathsome nymph. Her hand rose to strike...

And Zeus hurled magic like a thunderbolt,
so that where, a moment before, Callisto
had been running, now a great brown bear
ambled through the groves of Olympus,
soft-furred and round with unborn cub.

Too late. Hera had seen the
transformation. "Do you suppose you will
save her that way?" asked Hera, spiteful
with scorn. She cupped her hands round
her mouth and called down to her friend.

"Artemis! Oh, Artemis dear! Do you see?
A *bear* is loose in your hunting ground.
A dangerous *bear* is loose!"

The bear quickened its loping stride.
It cast its brown eyes towards Heaven
and whined softly. It ran through rivers
in a burst of shining spray. It loped uphill
towards the dusk-darkening sky. Behind
it came Artemis the huntress, with
Actaeon's hounds at her heels and
her maidens, running. The bear reached
the very gates of the Cloudy Citadel.

But Hera had locked them.
Callisto the bear reared
up on her hind paws
and turned to meet
the dogs and the
arrows of Artemis.
Hera leant eagerly
out of the windows
of Heaven, to
watch the sport.

But behind her a voice said, "Do you
suppose you will destroy her that way?
Do you really suppose you are more
powerful than Shining Zeus?"

And Zeus threw magic like sheet
lightning, so that the bear Callisto
leapt high into the sky, dissolving into
a furry blackness outlined in stars.

Soon afterwards, when the constellation
of the Great Bear rose into
the night sky, a
smaller star group
followed her –
Callisto's bear-cub
son. And though
Artemis still
shoots at mother and
child, her arrows
fall harmlessly back
to Earth, because
the Great and
Little Bear are
made of the
night air.

From her starry park in Heaven, Callisto and Arcas have witnessed the small lives and the great events of history. The first sight they saw was a pair of twin eagles meeting in the sky, dropping down to perch on a pillar of stone. Zeus's eagles had found the centre of the world.